Scientific Advertising

by

Claude C. Hopkins

Qurate
quratebooks.com

SCIENTIFIC ADVERTISING

Claude C. Hopkins

Published by Qurate Books Pvt. Ltd.

Published in 2024

ISBN: 978-93-58987-88-1

Qurate Books Pvt. Ltd.
Goa 403523, India
www.quratebooks.com
Tel: 1800-210-6527, Email: info@quratebooks.com

Contents

Chapter One- How Advertising Laws are Established 5
Chapter Two -Just Salesmanship 10
Chapter Three- Offer Service 14
Chapter Four- Mail Order Advertising - What it Teaches 17
Chapter Five- Headlines 22
Chapter Six- Psychology 27
Chapter Seven- Being Specific 32
Chapter Eight- Tell Your Full Story 36
Chapter Nine- Art in Advertising 40
Chapter Ten- Things Too Costly 44
Chapter Eleven- Information 49
Chapter Twelve- Strategy 52
Chapter Thirteen- Use of Samples 56
Chapter Fourteen- Getting Distribution 62
Chapter Fifteen- Test Campaigns 66
Chapter Sixteen- Leaning on Dealers 71
Chapter Seventeen- Individuality 74
Chapter Eighteen- Negative Advertising 76
Chapter Nineteen- Letter Writing 78
Chapter Twenty- A Name that Helps 81
Chapter Twenty-One- Good Business 83

Chapter One

How Advertising Laws are Established

The time has come when advertising has in some hands reached the status of a science. It is based on fixed principles and is reasonably exact. The causes and effects have been analyzed until they are well understood.

The correct methods of procedure have been proved and established. We know what is most effective, and we act on basic law.

Advertising, once a gamble, has thus become, under able direction, one of the safest business ventures. Certainly no other enterprise with comparable possibilities need involve so little risk.

Therefore, this book deals, not with theories and opinions, but with well-proven principles and facts. It is written as a text book for students and a safe guide for advertisers.

Every statement has been weighed. The book is confined to establish fundamentals. If we enter any realms of uncertainty we shall carefully denote them.

The present status of advertising is due to many reasons. Much national advertising has long been handled by large organizations known as advertising agencies. Some of these agencies, in their hundreds of campaigns, have tested and compared thousands of plans and ideas.

The results have been watched and recorded, so no lessons have been lost.

Such agencies employ a high grade of talent. None but able and experienced men can meet the requirements in national advertising.

Working in co-operation, learning from each other and from each new undertaking, some of these men develop into masters.

Individuals may come and go, but they leave their records and ideas behind them. These become a part of the organization's equipment, and a guide to all who follow.

Thus, in the course of decades, such agencies become storehouses of advertising experiences, proved principles, and methods.

The larger agencies also come into intimate contact with experts in every department of business. Their clients are usually dominating concerns. So they see the results of countless methods and policies. They become a clearing house for everything pertaining to merchandising.

Nearly every selling question which arises in business is accurately answered by many experiences.

Under these conditions, where they long exist, advertising and merchandising become exact sciences. Every course is charted. The compass of accurate knowledge directs the shortest, safest, cheapest course to any destination.

We learn the principles and prove them by repeated tests. This is done through keyed advertising, by traced returns, largely by the use of coupons. We compare one way with many others, backward and forward, and record the results.

When one method invariably proves best, that method becomes a fixed principle.

Mail order advertising is traced down to the fraction of a penny. The cost per reply and cost per dollar of sale show up with utter exactness. One ad in compared with another, one method with another. Headlines, settings, sizes, arguments and pictures are compared. To reduce the cost of results even one percent means much in some mail order advertising. So no guesswork is permitted. One must know what is best. Thus mail order advertising first established many of our basic laws.

In lines where direct returns are impossible, we compare one town with another. Scores of methods may be compared in this way, measured by cost of sales.

But the most common way is by use of the coupon. We offer a sample, a book, a free package, or something to induce direct replies. Thus we learn the amount of action which each ad engenders.

But those figures are not final. One ad may bring too many worthless replies, another, replies that are valuable. So our final conclusions are always based on cost per customer or cost per dollar of sale.

These coupon plans are dealt with further in the chapter on "Test Campaigns." Here we explain only how we employ them to discover advertising principles.

In a large agency coupon returns are watched and recorded on hundreds of different lines. In a single line they are sometimes recorded on thousands of separate ads. Thus we test everything pertaining to advertising. We answer nearly every possible question by multitudinous traced returns.

Some things we learn in this way apply only to particular lines. But even those supply basic principles for analogous undertakings.

Others apply to all lines. They become fundamentals for advertising in general. They are universally applied. No wise advertiser will ever depart from those unvarying laws.

We propose in this book to deal with those fundamentals, those universal principles. To teach only established techniques. There is that technique in advertising, as in all art, science and mechanics. And it is, as in all lines, a basic essential.

The lack of those fundamentals has been the main trouble with advertising of the past. Each worker was a law to himself. All previous knowledge, all progress in the line, was a closed book to him.

It was like a man trying to build a modern locomotive without first ascertaining what others had done. It was like a Columbus starting out to find an undiscovered land. Men were guided by whims and fancies - vagrant, changing breezes. They rarely arrived at their port.

When they did - by accident - it was by a long roundabout course. Each early mariner in this sea mapped his own separate course. There were no charts to guide him.

Not a lighthouse marked a harbor, not a buoy showed a reef. The wrecks were unrecorded, so countless ventures came to grief on the same rocks and shoals.

Advertising was then a gamble - a speculation of the rashest sort. One man's guess on the proper course was as likely to be as good as another's. There were no safe pilots, because few sailed the same course twice.

The condition has been corrected. Now the only uncertainties pertain to people and to products, not to methods. It is hard to measure human idiosyncrasies, the preferences and prejudices, the likes and dislikes that exist.

We cannot say that an article will be popular, but we know how to sell it in the most effective way. Ventures may fail, but the failures are not disasters. Losses, when they occur, are but trifling. And the causes are factors which have nothing to do with the advertising.

Advertising has flourished under these new conditions. It has multiplied in volume, in prestige and respect. The perils have increased many-fold. Just because the gamble has become a science, the speculation a very conservative business.

These facts should be recognized by all. This is no proper field for sophistry or theory, or for any other will-o'-the-wisp. The blind leading the blind is ridiculous.

It is pitiful in a field with such vast possibilities. Success is a rarity, a maximum success an impossibility, unless one is guided by laws as immutable as the law of gravitation.

So our main purpose here is to set down those laws, and to tell you how to prove them for yourself. After them come a myriad variations.

No two advertising campaigns are ever conducted on lines that are identical.

Individuality is an essential. Imitation is a reproach.

But those variable things which depend on ingenuity have not place in a text book on advertising. This is for groundwork only.

Ourhopeistofosteradvertisingthroughabetterunderstanding. To place it on a business basis. To have it recognized as among the safest, surest ventures which lead to large returns. Thousands of conspicuous successes show its possibilities.

Their variety points out its almost unlimited scope. Yet thousands who need it - who can never attain their deserts without it - still look upon its accomplishments as somewhat accidental.

That was so, but it is not so now. We hope that this book will throw some new lights on the subject.

Chapter Two

Just Salesmanship

To properly understand advertising or to learn even its rudiments one must start with the right conception. Advertising is salesmanship. Its principles are the principles of salesmanship.

Successes and failures in both lines are due to like causes. Thus every advertising question should be answered by the salesman's standards.

Let us emphasize that point. The only purpose of advertising is to make sales. It is profitable or unprofitable according to its actual sales. It is not for general effect. It is not to keep your name before the people. It is not primarily to aid your other salesmen.

Treat it as a salesman. Force it to justify itself. Compare it with other salesmen. Figure its cost and result. Accept no excuses which good salesmen do not make. Then you will not go far wrong.

The difference is only in degree. Advertising is multiplied salesmanship. It may appeal to thousands while the salesman talks to one. It involves a corresponding cost. Some people spend $10 per word on an average advertisement. Therefore every ad should be a super - salesman.

A salesman's mistake may cost little. An advertiser's mistake may cost a thousand times that much. Be more cautious, more exacting, therefore. A mediocre salesman may affect a small part of your trade. Mediocre advertising affects all of your trade.

Many think of advertising as ad-writing. Literary qualifications have no more to do with it than oratory has with salesmanship. One must be able to express himself briefly, clearly and convincingly, just as a salesman must.

But fine writing is a distinct disadvantage. So is unique literary style. They take attention from the subject. They reveal the hook. Any studied attempt to sell, if apparent, creates corresponding resistance.

That is so in personal salesmanship as in salesmanship-in-print. Fine talkers are rarely good salesman. They inspire buyers with the fear of over-influence. They create the suspicion that an effort is made to sell them on other lines than merit.

Successful salesmen are rarely good speech makers. They have few oratorical graces. They are plain and sincere men who know their customers and know their lines.

So it is in ad-writing. Many of the ablest men in advertising are graduate salesmen. The best we know have been house-to-house canvassers. They may know little of grammar, nothing of rhetoric, but they know how to use words that convince.

There is one simple way to answer many advertising questions.

Ask yourself, "Would it help a salesman sell the goods?"

"Would it help me sell them if I met a buyer in person?"

A fair answer to those questions avoids countless mistakes. But when one tries to show off, or does things merely to please himself, he is little likely to strike a chord which leads people to spend money.

Some argue for slogans, some like clever conceits. Would you use them in personal salesmanship? Can you imagine a customer whom such things would impress? If not, don't rely on them for selling in print.

Some say "Be very brief. People will read for little." Would you say that to a salesman? With a prospect standing before him, would you confine him to any certain number of words? That would be an unthinkable handicap.

So in advertising. The only readers we get are people whom our subject interests. No one reads ads for amusement, long or short. Consider them as prospects standing before you, seeking for information. Give them enough to get action.

Some advocate large type and big headlines. Yet they do not admire salesmen who talk in loud voices. People read all they care to read in 8-point type. Our magazines and newspapers are printed in that type. Folks are accustomed to it.

Anything louder is like loud conversation. It gains no attention worthwhile. It may not be offensive, but it is useless and wasteful. It multiplies the cost of your story. And to many it seems loud and blatant.

Others look for something queer and unusual. They want ads distinctive in style or illustration. Would you want that in a salesman? Do not men who act and dress in normal ways make a far better impression?.

Some insist in dressy ads. That is all right to a certain degree, but is quite important. Some poorly dressed men, prove to be excellent salesmen. Overdress in either is a fault.

So with countless questions. Measure them by salesmen's standards, not by amusement standards. Ads are not written to entertain. When they do, those entertainment seekers are little likely to be the people whom you want.

That is one of the greatest advertising faults. Ad writers abandon their parts. They forget they are salesmen and try to be performers. Instead of sales, they seek applause.

When you plan or prepare an advertisement, keep before you a typical buyer. Your subject, your headline has gained his or her attention. Then in everything be guided by what you would do if you met the buyer face-to-face. If you are a normal man and a good salesman you will then do your level best.

Don't think of people in the mass. That gives you a blurred view. Think of a typical individual, man or women, who is likely to want what you sell. Don't try to be amusing. Money spending is a serious matter.

Don't boast, for all people resent it. Don't try to show off. Do just what you think a good salesman should do with a half-sold person before him.

Some advertising men go out in person and sell to people before they plan to write an ad. One of the ablest of them has spent weeks on one article, selling from house to house.

In this way they learn the reactions from different forms of argument and approach. They learn what possible buyers want and the factors which don't appeal. It is quite customary to interview hundreds of possible customers.

Others send out questionnaires to learn the attitude of the buyers. In some way all must learn how to strike responsive chords. Guesswork is very expensive.

The maker of an advertised article knows the manufacturing side and probably the dealer's side. But this very knowledge often leads him astray in respect to customers. His interests are not in their interests.

The advertising man studies the consumer. He tries to place himself in the position of the buyer. His success largely depends on doing that to the exclusion of everything else.

This book will contain no more important chapter than this one on salesmanship. The reason for most of the non-successes in advertising is trying to sell people what they do not want. But next to that comes lack of true salesmanship.

Ads are planned and written with some utterly wrong conception. They are written to please the seller. The interest of the buyer is forgotten. One can never sell goods profitable, in person or in print, when that attitude exists.

Chapter Three

Offer Service

Remember the people you address are selfish, as we all are. They care nothing about your interests or your profit. They seek service for themselves. Ignoring this fact is a common mistake and a costly mistake in advertising. Ads say in effect, "Buy my brand. Give me the trade you give to others. Let me have the money." That is not a popular appeal.

The best ads ask no one to buy. That is useless. Often they do not quote a price. They do not say that dealers handle the product.

The ads are based entirely on service. They offer wanted information. They cite advantages to users. Perhaps they offer a sample, or a place to buy the first package, or to send something on approval, so the customer may prove the claims without any cost or risks.

Some of these ads seem altruistic. But they are based on the knowledge of human nature. The writers know how people are led to buy.

Here again is salesmanship. The good salesman does not merely cry a name. He doesn't say, "Buy my article." He pictures the customer's side of his service until the natural result is to buy.

A brush maker has some 2,000 canvassers who sells brushes from house to house. He is enormously successful in a line which would seem very difficult. And it would be for his men if they asked the housewives to buy. But they don't.

They go to the door and say, "I was sent here to give you a brush. I have samples here and I want you to take your choice."

The housewife is all smiles and attention. In picking out one brush she sees several she wants. She is also anxious to reciprocate the gift. So the salesman gets an order.

Another concern sells coffee, etc., by wagons in some 500 cities. The man drops in with a half- pound of coffee and says, "Accept this package and try it. I'll come back in a few days to ask you how you liked it."

Even when he comes back he doesn't ask for an order. He explains that he wants to send the women a fine kitchen utensil. It isn't free, but if she likes the coffee he will credit five cents on each pound she buys until she has paid for the article. Always some service.

The maker of the electric sewing machine motor found advertising difficult. So, on good advice, he ceased soliciting a purchase. He offered to send to any home, through any dealer, a motor for one week's use. With it would come a man to show her how to operate it.

"Let us help you for a week without cost or obligation," said the ad. Such an offer was resistless, and about nine in ten of the trials led to sales.

So in many, many lines. Cigar makers send out boxes to anyone and say, "Smoke ten, then keep them or return them, as you wish."

Makers of books, typewriters, washing machines, kitchen cabinets, vacuum sweepers, etc., send out their products without any prepayment.

They say, "Use them a week, then do as you wish."

Practically all merchandise sold by mail is sent subject to return.

These are all common principles of salesmanship. The most ignorant peddler applies them. Yet the salesman-in-print very often forgets them.

He talks about his interest. He blazons a name, as though that was of importance. His phrase is, "Drive people to the stores," and that is his attitude in everything he says.

People can be coaxed but not driven.

Whatever they do they do to please themselves.

Many fewer mistakes would be made in advertising if these facts were never forgotten.

Chapter Four

Mail Order Advertising - What it Teaches

The severest test of an advertising man is in selling goods by mail. But that is a school from which he must graduate before he can hope for success. There cost and result is immediately apparent.

False theories melt away like snowflakes in the sun. The advertising is profitable or it is not, clearly on the face of returns. Figures which do not lie, tell one at once the merits of an ad.

This puts men on their mettle. All guesswork is eliminated. Every mistake is conspicuous. One quickly loses his conceit by learning how often his judgment errs - often nine times in ten.

There one learns that advertising must be done on a scientific basis to have any fair chance of success. And he learns that every wasted dollar adds to the cost of results.

Here he is taught tough efficiency and economy under a master who can't be fooled. Then, and only then, is he apt to apply the same principles and keys to all advertising.

A man was selling a $5 article. The replies from his ad cost him 85 cents. Another man submitted an ad which he thought better. The replies cost $14.20 each. Another man submitted an ad which for two years brought replies at an average of 41 cents each.

Consider the difference, on 250,000 replies per year. Think how valuable was the man who cut the cost in two. Think what it would have meant to continue that $14.20 ad without any key on returns.

Yet there are thousands of advertisers who do just that. They spend large sums on a guess. And they are doing what that man did - paying for sales from 2 to 35 times what they need cost.

A study of mail order advertising reveals many things worth learning. It is a prime subject for study. In the first place, if continued, you know that it pays. It is therefore good advertising as applied to that line.

The probability is that the ad has resulted from many traced comparisons. It is therefore the best advertising, not theoretical. It will not deceive you. The lessons it teaches are principles which wise men apply to all advertising.

Mail order advertising is always set in small type. It is usually set in smaller type than ordinary print. That economy of space is universal. So it proves conclusively that larger type does not pay.

Remember that, when you double your space by doubling the size of your type. The ad may still be profitable. But traced returns have proved that you are paying a double price for sales.

In mail order advertising there is no waste of space. Every line is utilized. Borders are rarely used. Remember that, when you are tempted to leave valuable space unoccupied.

In mail order advertising there is no jargon. There is no boasting, save of super-service. There is no useless talk. There is no attempt at entertainment. There is nothing to amuse.

Mail order advertising usually contains a coupon. That is there to cut out as a reminder of something the reader has decided to do.

Mail order advertisers know that readers forget. They are reading a magazine of interest. They may be absorbed in a story.

A large percentage of people who read and ad and decide to act, will forget that decision in five minutes.

The mail order advertiser knows that waste by tests, and he does not propose to accept it. So he inserts that reminder to be cut out, and it turns up when the reader is ready to act.

In mail order advertising the pictures are always to the point. They are salesmen in themselves. They earn space they occupy. The size is gauged by their importance. The picture of a dress one is trying to sell may occupy much space. Less important things get smaller spaces.

Pictures in ordinary advertising may teach little. They probably result in whims. But pictures in mail order advertising may form half the cost of selling.

And you may be sure that everything about them has been decided by many comparative tests. Before you use useless pictures, merely to decorate or interest, look over some mail order ads. Mark what their verdict is.

A man advertised an incubator to be sold by mail. Type ads with right headlines brought excellent returns. But he conceived the idea that a striking picture would increase those returns. So he increased his space 50 per cent to add a row of chickens in silhouette.

It did make a striking ad, but his cost per reply was increased by exactly that 50 per cent. The new ad, costing one-half more for every insertion, brought not one added sale.

The man learned that incubator buyers were practical people. They were looking for attractive offers, not for pictures.

Think of the countless untraced campaigns where a whim of that kind costs half the advertising money without a penny in return. And it may go on year after year.

Mail order advertising tells a complete story if the purpose is to make an immediate sale. You see no limitations there on amount of copy.

The motto there is, "The more you tell the more you sell."

And it has never failed to prove out so in any test we know.

Sometimes the advertiser uses small ads, sometimes large ads. None are too small to tell a reasonable story. But an ad twice larger brings twice the returns. A four-times-larger ad brings four times the returns, and usually some in addition.

But this occurs only when the larger space is utilized as well as the small space. Set half-page copy in a page space and you double the cost in returns. We have seen many a test prove that.

Look at an ad of the Mead Cycle Company - a typical mail order ad. These have been running for many years. The ads are unchanging. Mr. Mead told the writer that not for $10,000 would he change a single word in his ads.

For many years he compared one ad with the other. And the ads you see today are the final results of all those experiments. Note the picture he uses, the headlines, the economy of space, the small type. Those ads are as near perfect for their purpose as an ad can be.

So with any other mail order ad which has long continued. Every feature, every word and picture teaches advertising at its best.

You may not like them. You may say they are unattractive, crowded, hard to read - anything you will. But the test of results has proved those ads the best salesman those lines have yet discovered. And they certainly pay.

Mail order advertising is the court of last resort. You may get the same instruction, if you will, by keying other ads.

But mail order ads are models. They are selling goods profitably in a difficult way. It is far harder to get mail orders than to send buyers to the stores.

It is hard to sell goods which can't be seen. Ads which do that are excellent examples of what advertising should be.

We cannot often follow all the principles of mail order advertising, though we know we should. The advertiser forces a compromise. Perhaps pride in our ads has an influence.

But every departure from those principles adds to our selling cost. Therefore it is always a question of what we are willing to pay for our frivolities.

We can at least know what we pay. We can make keyed comparisons, one ad with another. Whenever we do we invariably find that the nearer we get to proved mail order copy the more customers we get for our money.

This is another important chapter. Think it over.

What real difference is there between inducing a customer to order by mail or order from his dealer? Why should the methods of salesmanship differ?

They should not.

When they do, it is for one of two reasons. Either the advertiser does not know what the mail order advertiser knows, or he is advertising blindly.

Or he is deliberately sacrificing a percentage of his returns to gratify some desire.

There is some apology for that, just as there is for fine offices and buildings.

Most of us can afford to do something for pride and opinion.

But let us know what we are doing. Let us know the cost of our pride.

Then, if our advertising fails to bring us the wanted returns, let us go back to our model - a good mail order ad - and eliminate some of our waste.

Chapter Five

Headlines

The difference between advertising and personal salesmanship lies largely in personal contact. The salesman is there to demand attention. He cannot be ignored.

The advertisement can be ignored.

But the salesman wastes much of his time on prospects whom he can never hope to interest. He cannot pick them out. The advertisement is read only by interested people who, by their own volition, study what we have to say.

The purpose of headline is to pick out people you can interest. You wish to talk to someone in a crowd. So the first thing you say is, "Hey there, Bill Jones" to get the right persons attention.

The same in an advertisement. What you have will interest certain people only, and for certain reasons. You care only for those people, so create a headline which will hail those people only!

Perhaps a blind headline or some clever conceit will attract many times as many. But they may consist of mostly impossible subjects for what you have to offer. And the people you are after may never realize that the ad refers to something they may want.

Headlines on ads are like headlines on news items. Nobody reads a whole newspaper. One is interested in financial news, one in political, one in society, one in cookery, one in sports, etc.

There are whole pages in any newspaper which we may never scan at all. Yet other people might turn directly to those pages. We pick out what we wish to read by headlines, and we don't want those headlines misleading.

The writing of headlines is one of the greatest journalistic arts. They either conceal or reveal an interest.

Suppose a newspaper article stated that a certain woman was the most beautiful in the city. That article would be of intense interest to that woman and her friends. But neither she nor her friends would ever read it if the headline was "Egyptian Psychology."

So in advertising.

It is commonly said that people do not read advertisements.

That is silly, of course. We who spend millions in advertising and watch the returns marvel at the readers we get.

Again and again we see 20 per cent of all the readers of a newspaper cut out a certain coupon.

But people do not read ads for amusement. They don't read ads which, at a glance, seem to offer nothing interesting.

A double-page ad on women's dresses will not gain a glance from a man. Nor will shaving cream ad from a woman.

Always bear these facts in mind. People are hurried. The average person worth cultivating has too much to read. They skip three-fourths of the reading matter which they pay to get.

They are not going to read your business talk unless you make it worth their while and let the headline show it.

People will not be bored in print. They may listen politely at a dinner table to boasts and personalities, life history, etc. But in print they choose their own companions, their own subjects.

They want to be amused or benefited. They want economy, beauty, labor saving, good things to eat and wear. There may be products which interest them more than anything else in the magazine. But they will never know it unless the headline or picture tells them.

The writer of this chapter spends far more time on headlines that on writing, He often spends hours on a single headline. Often scores of headlines are discarded before the right one is selected.

For the entire return from an ad depends on attracting the right sort of readers. The best of salesmanship has no chance whatever unless we get a hearing.

The vast difference in headlines is shown by keyed returns which this book advocates. The identical ad run with various headlines differs tremendously in its returns.

It is not uncommon for a change in headlines to multiply returns from five or ten times over. So we compare headlines until we know what sort of appeal pays best. That differs in every line, of course.

The writer has before him keyed returns on nearly two thousand headlines used on a single product. The story in these ads are nearly identical. But the returns vary enormously, due solely to the headlines. So with every keyed return in our record appear the headlines that we used.

Thus we learn what type of headline has the most wide-spread appeal. The product has many uses. It fosters beauty. It prevents disease. It aides daintiness and cleanliness. We learn to exactness which quality most of our readers seek.

That does not mean we neglect the others.

One sort of appeal may bring half the returns of another, yet be important enough to be profitable.

We overlook no field that pays. But we know what proportion of our ads should, in the headline, attract any certain class.

For this same reason we employ a vast variety of ads. If we are using twenty magazines we may use twenty separate ads.

This is because circulation's overlap, and because a considerable percentage of people are attracted by each of several forms of approach.

We wish to reach them all.

On soap, for instance, the headline "Keep Clean" might attract a very small percentage. It is to common place.

So might the headline, "No animal fat." People may not care much about that.

The headline, "It floats" might prove interesting.

But a headline referring to beauty or complexion might attract many times as many.

An automobile ad might refer in the headline to a good universal joint. It might fall flat, because so few buyers think of universal joints.

The same ad with a headline, "The Sportiest of Sport Bodies," might out-pull the other fifty to one. This is enough to suggest the importance of headlines.

Anyone who keys ads will be amazed at the difference.

The appeals we like best will rarely prove best, because we do not know enough people to average up their desires. So we learn on each line by experiment.

But back of all, lie fixed principles.

You are presenting an ad to millions.

Among them is a percentage, small or large, whom you hope to interest.

Go after that percentage and try to strike the chord that responds. If you are advertising corsets, men and children don't interest you.

If you are advertising cigars, you have no use for non-smokers.

Razors won't attract women, and rouge will not interest men.

Don't think that those millions will read your ads to find out if your product interests. They will decide by a glance - by your headline or your pictures.

Address the people you seek, and address them only.

Chapter Six

Psychology

The competent advertising man must understand psychology. The more he knows about it the better. He must learn that certain effects lead to certain reactions, and use that knowledge to increase results and avoid mistakes.

Human nature is perpetual. In most respects it is the same today as in the time of Caesar. So the principles of psychology are fixed and enduring. You will never need to unlearn what you learn about them.

We learn, for instance, that curiosity is one of the strongest human incentives. We employ it whenever we can.

Puffed Wheat and Puffed Rice were made successful largely through curiosity. "Grains puffed to 8 times the normal size." "Foods shot from guns." "125 million steam explosions caused in every kernel."

These foods were failures before that factor was discovered.

We learn that cheapness is not a strong appeal. Americans are extravagant. They want bargains but not cheapness. They want to feel that they can afford to eat and have and wear the best.

Treat them as if they could not, and they resent your attitude.

We learn that people judge largely by price. They are not experts. In the British National Gallery is a painting which is announced in a catalog to have cost $750,000. Most people at first pass it by at a glance. Then later they get farther on in the catalog and learn what the painting cost. They return then and surround it.

A department store advertised at one Easter time a $1,000 hat, and the floor could not hold the women who came to see it.

We often employ this factor in psychology. Perhaps we are advertising a valuable formula. To merely say that would not be impressive. So we state - as a fact - that we paid $100,000 for that formula. That statement, when tried, has won a wealth of respect.

Many articles are sold under guarantee - so commonly sold that guarantees have ceased to be impressive. But one concern made a fortune by offering a dealer's signed warrant.

The dealer to whom one paid his money agreed in writing to pay it back if asked. Instead of a far-away stranger, a neighbor gave the warrant. The results have led many to try that plan, and it has always proved effective.

Many have advertised, "Try it for a week. If you don't like it we'll return your money."

Then someone conceived the idea of sending goods without any money down, and saying, "Pay in a week if you like them." That proved many times impressive.

One great advertising man stated the difference this way:

"Two men came to me, each offering me a horse. Both made equal claims. They were good horses, kind and gentle. A child could drive them.

One man said, 'Try the horse for a week. If my claims are not true, come back for your money.' The other man also said, 'Try the horse for week.' But he added, 'Come and pay me then.' I naturally bought the second man's horse."

Now countless things - cigars, typewriters, washing machines, books, etc. - are sent out in this way on approval. And we find that people are honest. The losses are very small.

An advertiser offered a set of books to business men. The advertising was unprofitable, so he consulted another expert. The ads were impressive. The offer seemed attractive.

"But," said the second man, "let us add one little touch which I have found effective. Let us offer to put the buyer's name in gilt lettering on each book." That was done, and with scarcely another change in the ads they sold some hundreds of thousands of books.

Through some peculiar kink in human psychology that names in gilt gave much added value to the books.

Many send out small gifts, like memorandum books, to customers and prospects. They get very small results. One man sent out a letter to the effect that he had a leather-covered book with a man's name on it. It was waiting on him and would be sent on request.

The form of request was enclosed, and it also asked for certain information. That information indicated lines on which a man might be sold.

Nearly all men, it was found, filled out that request that and supplied the information. When a man knows that something belongs to them - something with his name on - he will make an effort to get it, even though the thing is a trifle.

In the same way it is found that an offer limited to a certain class of people is far more effective than a general offer. For instance, an offer limited to veterans of the war. Or to members of a lodge or sect. Or to executives. Those who are entitled to any seeming advantage will go a long way not to lose that advantage.

An advertiser suffered much from substitution. He said, "Look out for substitutes," "Be sure you get this brand," etc., with no effect. Those were selfish appeals.

Then he said, "Try our rivals' too" - said it in his headlines. He invited comparisons and showed that he did not fear them. That corrected the situation. Buyers were careful to get the brand so conspicuously superior that its maker could court a trial of the rest.

Two advertisers offered food products nearly identical. Both offered a full-size package as an introduction. But one gave his package free. The other bought the package. A coupon was good at any store for a package, for which the maker paid retail price.

The first advertiser failed and the second succeeded. The first even lost a large part of the trade he had. He cheapened his product by giving a 15-cent package away. It is hard to pay for an article which has once been free. It is like paying railroad fare after traveling on a pass.

The other gained added respect for his article by paying retail price to let the user try it. An article good enough for the maker to buy is good enough for the user to buy. It is vastly different to pay 15 cents to let you try an article that to simply say "It's free.".

So with sampling. Hand an unwanted product to a housewife and she pays it slight respect. She is in no mood to see its virtues. But get her to ask for a sample after reading your story, and she is in a very different position. She knows your claims. She is interested in them, else she would not act. And she expects to find the qualities you told.

There is a great deal in mental impression. Submit five articles exactly alike and five people may choose one of them. But point out in one some qualities to notice and everyone will find them. The five people then will all choose the same article.

If people can be made sick or well by mental impressions, they can be made to favor a certain brand in that way. And that, on some lines, is the only way to win them.

Two concerns, side by side, sold women's clothing on installments. The appeal, of course, was to poor girls who desire to dress better. One treated them like poor girls and made the bare business offer.

The other put a woman in charge - a motherly, dignified, capable woman. They did business in her name. They used her picture. She signed all ads and letters. She wrote to these girls like a friend.

She knew herself what it meant to a girl not to be able to dress her best. She had long sought a chance to supply women good clothes and give them all season to pay. Now she was able to do so, with the aid of men behind her.

There was no comparison in those two appeals. It was not long before this woman's long - established next-door rival had to quit.

The backers of this business sold house furnishings on installments. Sending out catalogs promiscuously did not pay. Offering long-time credit often seems like a reflection.

But when a married woman bought garments from Mrs. X, and paid as agreed, they wrote to her something like this: "Mrs. X, whom we know, tells us that you are one of her good customers. She has dealt with you, she says, and you do just as you agree.

So we have opened with you a credit account on our books, good any time you wish. When you want anything in furnishings, just order it. Pay nothing in advance. We are very glad to send it without any investigation to a person recommended as you are."

That was flattering. Naturally those people, when they wanted some furniture, would order from that house.

There are endless phases to psychology. Some people know them by instinct. Many of them are taught by experience. But we learn most of them from others. When we see a winning method we note it down for use when occasion offers.

These things are very important. An identical offer made in a different way may bring multiplied returns. Somewhere in the mines of business experience we must find the best method somehow.

Chapter Seven

Being Specific

Platitudes and generalities roll off the human understanding like water from a duck. They leave no impression whatever. To say, "Best in the world," "Lowest price in existence," etc. are at best simply claiming the expected.

But superlatives of that sort are usually damaging. They suggest looseness of expression, a tendency to exaggerate, a careless truth. They lead readers to discount all the statements that you make.

People recognize a certain license in selling talk as they do poetry. A man may say, "Supreme in quality" without seeming a liar, though one may know that the other brands are equally as good. One expects a salesman to put his best foot forward and excuses some exaggeration born of enthusiasm. But just for that reason general statements count for little. And a man inclined to superlatives must expect that his every statement will be taken with some caution.

But a man who makes a specific claim is either telling the truth or a lie.

People do not expect an advertiser to lie. They know that he can't lie in the best mediums.

The growing respect in advertising has largely come through a growing regard for its truth. So a definite statement is usually accepted.

Actual figures are not generally discounted. Specific facts, when stated, have their full weight and effect.

This is very important to consider in written or personal salesmanship. The weight of an argument may often be multiplied by making it specific.

Say that a tungsten lamp gives more light than a carbon and you leave some doubt. Say it gives three and one-third times the light and people realize that you have made tests and comparisons.

A dealer may say, "Our prices have been reduced" without creating any marked impression. But when he says, "Our prices have been reduced 25 per cent" he gets the full value of his announcement.

A mail order advertiser sold women's clothing to people of the poorer classes. For years he used the slogan, "Lowest prices in America." His rivals all copied that.

Then he guaranteed to undersell any other dealer. His rivals did likewise. Soon those claims became common to every advertiser in his line, and they became commonplace.

Then under able advice, he changed his statement to "Our net profit is 3 %." That was a definite statement and it proved very impressive. With their volume of business it was evident that their prices must be minimum. No one could be expected to do business on less than 3 per cent. The next year their business made a sensational increase.

At one time in the automobile business there was a general impression that profits were excessive. One well-advised advertiser came out with this statement, "Our profit is 9 per cent." Then he cited actual costs on the hidden costs of a $1,500 car. They amounted to $735, without including anything one could easily see. This advertiser made a great success along those lines at that time.

Shaving soaps have long been advertised "Abundant lather," "Does not dry on the face," "Acts quickly," etc. One advertiser had as good a chance as the other to impress those claims.

Then a new maker came into the field. It was a tremendously difficult field, for every customer had to be taken from someone else. He stated specific facts.

He said, "Softens the beard in one minute" and

"Maintains its creamy fullness for ten minutes on the face."

"The final result of testing and comparing 130 formulas."

Perhaps never in advertising has there been a quicker and greater success in an equally difficult field.

Makers of safety razors have long advertised quick shaves. One maker advertised a 78-second shave. That was definite. It indicated actual tests. That man at once made a sensational advance in his sales.

In the old days all beers were advertised as "Pure." The claim made no impression. The bigger the type used, the bigger the folly.

After millions had been spent to impress a platitude, one brewer pictured a plate glass where beer was cooled in filtered air. He pictured a filter of white wood pulp through which every drop was cleared. He told how bottles were washed four times by machinery.

How he went down 4,000 feet for pure water. How 1,018 experiments had been made to attain a yeast to give beer that matchless flavor. And how all the yeast was forever made from that adopted mother cell.

All claims were such as any brewer might have made. They were mere essentials in ordinary brewing. But he was the first to tell the people about them, while others cried merely "pure beer."

He made the greatest success that was ever made in beer advertising. "Used the world over" is a very elastic claim. Then one advertiser said, "Used by the peoples of 52 nations," and many others followed.

One statement may take as much room as another, yet a definite statement be many times as effective. The difference is vast.

If a claim is worth making, make it in the most impressive way.

All these effects must be studied. Salesmanship-in-print is very expensive. A salesman's loose talk matters little.

But when you are talking to millions at enormous cost, the weight of your claims is important.

No generality has any weight whatever. It is like saying, "How do you do?" when you have no intention of inquiring about one's health.

But specific claims when made in print are taken at their value.

Chapter Eight

Tell Your Full Story

Whatever claim you use to gain attention, the advertisement should tell a story reasonably complete. If you watch returns, you will find that certain claims appeal far more than others. But in usual lines, a number of claims appeal to a large percentage.

Then present those claims in every ad for their effect on that percentage.

Some advertisers, for sake of brevity, present one claim at a time. Or they write a serial ad, continued in another issue. There is no greater folly. Those serials almost never connect.

Once you get a person's attention, then is the time to accomplish all you ever hope with him. Bring all your good arguments to bear. Cover every phase of your subject.

One fact appeals to some, one to another. Omit any one and a certain percentage will lose the fact which might convince.

People are not apt to read successive advertisements on any single line. No more that you read a news item twice, or a story.

In one reading of an advertisement one decides for or against a proposition. And that operates against a second reading.

So present to the reader, when once you get him, every important claim you have.

The best advertisers do that. They learn their appealing claims by tests - by comparing results from various headlines. Gradually they accumulate a list a claims important enough to use. All those claims appear in every ad thereafter.

The advertisements seem monotonous to the men who read them all.

A complete story is always the same.

But one must consider that the average reader is only once a reader, probably. And what you fail to tell him in that ad is something he may never know.

Some advertisers go so far as to never change their ads. Single mail order ads often run year after year without diminishing returns.

So with some general ads. They are perfected ads, embodying in the best way known all that one has to say. Advertiser do not expect a second reading. Their constant returns come from getting new readers.

In every ad, consider only new customers. People using your product are not going to read your ads. They have already read and decided.

You might advertise month after month to present users that the product they use is poison, and they would never know it.

So never waste one line of your space to say something to present to users, unless you can say it in your headlines.

Bear in mind always that you can address an unconverted prospect.

Any reader of your ad is interested, else he would not be a reader. You are dealing with someone willing to listen.

So do your level best. That reader, if you lose him now, may never again be a reader.

You are like a salesman in a busy man's office. He may have tried again and again to gain entrance. He may never be admitted again. This is his one chance to get action, and he must employ it to the full.

This brings up the question of brevity. The most common expression you hear about advertising is that people will not read much.

Yet a vast amount of the best-paying advertising shows that people do read much. Then they write for a book, perhaps - for added information.

There is fixed rule on this subject of brevity.

One sentence may tell a complete story on a line like chewing gum. It may on an article like Cream of Wheat. But, whether long or short, an advertising story should be reasonably complete.

A certain man desired a personal car. He cared little about the price. He wanted a car to take pride in, else he felt he would never drive it. But, being a good business man, he wanted value for his money.

His inclination was towards a Rolls-Royce. He also considered a Pierce-Arrow, a Locomobile and others. But these famous cars offered no information. Their advertisements were very short.

Evidently the makers considered it undignified to argue comparative merits.

The Marmon, on the contrary, told a complete story. He read columns and books about it. So he bought a Marmon, and was never sorry.

But he afterwards learned facts about another car at nearly three times the price which would have sold him the car, had he known them.

What folly it is to cry a name in a line like that, plus a few brief generalities. A car may be a lifetime investment. It involves an important expenditure.

A man interested enough to buy a car will read a volume about it if the volume is interesting. So with everything.

You may be simply trying to change a woman from one breakfast food to another, or one tooth paste, or one soap. She is wedded to what she is using. Perhaps she has used it for years.

You have a hard proposition. If you do not believe it, go to her in person and try to make the change. Not to merely buy a first package to please you, but to adopt your brand.

A man who once does that at a woman's door won't argue for brief advertisements. He will never again say, "A sentence will do," or a name claim or a boast.

Nor will the man who traces his results.

Note that brief ads are never keyed.

Note that every traced ad tells a complete story, though it takes columns to tell.

Never be guided in any way by ads which are untraced.

Never do anything because some uninformed advertiser considers that something right. Never be led in new paths by the blind.

Apply to your advertising ordinary common sense. Take the opinion of nobody, whom knows nothing about his returns.

Chapter Nine

Art in Advertising

Pictures in advertising are very expensive. Not in cost of good artwork alone, but in the cost of space. From one-third to one-half of an advertising campaign is often staked on the power of the pictures.

Anything expensive must be effective, else it involves much waste. So art in advertising is a study of paramount importance.

Pictures should not be used merely because they are interesting, or to attract attention, or to decorate an ad.

We have covered these points elsewhere. Ads are not written to interest, please or amuse. You are not writing to please the hoi-polloi. You are writing on a serious subject - the subject of money-spending. And you address a restricted minority.

Use pictures only to attract those who may profit you. Use them only when they form a better selling argument than the same amount of space set in type.

Mail order advertisers, as we have said, have pictures down to a science. Some use large pictures, some small, some omit pictures entirely.

A noticeable fact is that none of them uses expensive art work. Be sure that all these things are done for reasons made apparent by results.

Any other advertiser should apply the same principles. Or, if none exist to apply to his line, he should work out his own by tests. It is certainly unwise to spend large sums on a dubious adventure.

Pictures in many lines form a major factor. Omitting the lines where the article itself should be pictured. In some lines, like Arrow Collars and most in clothing advertising, pictures have proved most convincing. Not only in picturing the collar or the clothes, but in picturing men whom others envy, in surroundings which others covet. The pictures subtly suggest that these articles of apparel will aid men to those desired positions.

So with correspondence schools. Theirs is traced advertising. Picturing men in high positions of taking upward steps forms a very convincing argument.

So with beauty articles. Picturing beautiful women, admired and attractive, is a supreme inducement. But there is a great advantage in including a fascinated man. Women desire beauty largely because of men. Then show them using their beauty, as women do use it, to gain maximum effect.

Advertising pictures should not be eccentric. Don't treat your subject lightly. Don't lessen respect for yourself or your article by any attempt at frivolity. People do not patronize a clown.

There are two things about which men should not joke. One is business, one is home. An eccentric picture may do you serious damage. One may gain attention by wearing a fool's cap. But he would ruin his selling prospects.

A picture which is eccentric or unique takes attention from your subject. You cannot afford to do that.

Your main appeal lies in headline. Over-shadow that and you kill it. Don't sacrifice the attention that you want, just to gain general and useless attention.

Don't be like a salesman who wears conspicuous clothes. The small percentage he appeals to are not usually good buyers. The great majority of the sane and thrifty heartily despite him.

Be normal in everything you do when you are seeking confidence and conviction. Generalities cannot be applied to art. There are seeming exceptions to most statements. Each line must be studied by itself.

But the picture must help sell the goods. It should help more than anything else could do in like space, else use that something else.

Many pictures tell a story better than type can do. In advertising of Puffed Grains the picture of the grains were found to be most effective. They awake curiosity. No figure drawing in that case compare in results with these grains.

Other pictures form a total loss. We have cited cases of that kind. The only way to know, as is with most other questions, is by compared results.

There are disputed questions in art work which we will cite without expressing opinions. They seem to be answered both ways, according to the line which is advertised.

Does it pay better to use fine art work or ordinary?

Some advertisers pay up to $2,000 per drawing. They figure that the space is expensive. The art cost is small in comparison. So they consider the best worth its cost.

Others argue that few people have art education. They bring out their ideas, and bring them out well, at a fraction of the cost. Mail order advertisers are generally in this class.

The question is one of small moment. Certainly good art pays as well as mediocre. And the cost of preparing ads is very small compared with the cost of insertion.

Should every ad have a new picture? Or may a picture be repeated? Both viewpoints have many supporters. The probability is that repetition is an economy.

We are after new customers always. It is not probable that they remember a picture we have used before. If they do, repetition does not detract.

Do color pictures pay better than black and white? Not generally, according to the evidence we have gathered to date. Yet there are exceptions.

Certain food dishes look far better in colors. Tests on lines like oranges, desserts, etc. show that color pays. Color comes close to placing the products on actual exhibition.

But color used to amuse or to gain attention is like anything else that we use for that purpose. It may attract many times as many people, yet not secure a hearing from as many whom we want.

The general rule applies. Do nothing to merely interest, amuse, or attract. That is not your province. Do only that which wins the people you are after in the cheapest possible way.

But these are minor questions. They are mere economies, not largely affecting the results of a campaign.

Some things you do may cut all your results in two. Other things can be done which multiply those results.

Minor costs are insignificant when compared with basic principles.

One man may do business in a shed, another in a palace. That is immaterial.

The great question is, one's power to get the maximum results.

Chapter Ten

Things Too Costly

Many things are possible in advertising which are too costly to attempt. That is another reason why every project and method should be weighed and determined by a known scale of cost and result.

Changing people's habits is very expensive. A project which involves that must be seriously considered.

To sell shaving soap to the peasants of Russia one would first need to change their beard wearing habits. The cost would be excessive, yet countless advertisers try to do things almost as impossible. Just because questions are not ably considered, and results are traced but unknown.

For instance, the advertiser of a dentifrice may spend much space and money to educate people to brush their teeth. Tests which we know of have indicated that the cost of such converts may run from $20 to $25 each. Not only because of the difficulty, but because much of the advertising goes to people already converted.

Such a cost, of course, is unthinkable. One might not in a lifetime get it back in sales. The maker who learned these facts by tests make no attempt to educate people to the tooth brush habit.

What cannot be done on a large scale profitably cannot be done on a small scale. So not one line in any ad is devoted to this object. This maker, who is constantly guided in everything by keying every ad, has made remarkable success.

Another dentifrice maker spends much money to make converts to the tooth brush. The object is commendable, but altruistic. The new business he creates is shared by his rivals. He is wondering why his sales increase is in no way commensurate with his expenditure.

An advertiser at one time spent much money to educate people to the use of oatmeal. The results were too small to discover. All people know of oatmeal. As a food for children it has age-old fame. Doctors have advised it for many generations.

People who don't serve oatmeal are therefore difficult to start. Perhaps their objections are insurmountable. Anyway, the cost proved to be beyond all possible return.

There are many advertisers who know facts like these and concede them. They would not think of devoting a whole campaign to any such impossible object.

Yet they devote a share of their space to that object. That is only the same folly on a smaller scale. It is not good business.

No one orange grower or raisin grower could attempt to increase the consumption of those fruits. The cost might be a thousand times his share of the returns. But thousands of growers combined have done it on those and many other lines.

There lies one of the great possibilities of advertising development. The general consumption of scores of foods can be profitably increased. But it must be done on wide co-operation.

No advertiser could afford to educate people on vitamins or germicides. Such things are done by authorities, through countless columns of unpaid-for space. But great successes have been made by going to people already educated and satisfying their created wants.

It is a very shrewd thing to watch the development of a popular trend, the creation of new desires. Then at the right time, offer to satisfy those desires. That was done on yeasts, for instance, and on numerous antiseptics.

It can every year be done on new things which some popular fashion or widespread influence is bring into vogue.

But it is a very different thing to create that fashion, taste or influence for all in your field to share.

There are some things we know of which might possibly be sold to half the homes in the country. A Dakin-fluid germicide, for instance. But the consumption would be very small. A small bottle might last for years. Customers might cost $1.50 each. And the revenue per customer might not in ten years repay the cost of getting them.

Mail order sales on single articles, however popular, rarely cost less than $2.50 each. It is reasonable to suppose that sales made through dealers on like articles will cost approximately as much. Those facts must be considered on any one-sale article. Possibly one user will win others. But traced returns as in mail order advertising would prohibit much advertising, which is now being done.

Costly mistakes are made by blindly following some ill-conceived idea. An article, for instance, may have many uses, one of which is to prevent disease. Prevention is not a popular subject, however much it should be.

People will do much to cure trouble, but people in general will do little to prevent it. This has been proved by many disappointments.

One may spend much money in arguing prevention when the same money spent on another claim would bring many times the sales. A heading which asserts one claim may bring ten times the results of a heading which asserted another. An advertiser may go far astray unless he finds out.

A tooth paste may tend to prevent decay. It may also beautify teeth. Tests will probably show that the latter appeal is many times as strong as the former.

The most successful tooth paste advertiser never features tooth troubles in his headlines. Tests have proved them unappealing. Other advertisers in this line center on those troubles. That is often because results are not known and compared.

A soap may tend to cure eczema. It may at the same time improve complexion. The eczema claim may appeal to one in a hundred while the beauty claims would appeal to nearly all. To even mention the eczema claims might destroy the beauty claims.

A man has a relief for asthma. It has done so much for him he considers it a great advertising possibility. We have no statistics on this subject. We do not know the percentage of people who suffer from asthma. A canvass might show it to be one in a hundred. If so, he would need to cover a hundred useless readers to reach one he wants.

His cost of result might be twenty times as high as on another article which appeals to one in five. That excessive cost would probably mean disaster. For reasons like these, every new advertiser should seek for wise advice. No one with the interests of advertising at heart will advise any dubious venture.

Some claims not popular enough to feature in the main are still popular enough to consider. They influence a certain number of people - say one-quarter of your possible customers.

Such claims may be featured to advantage in a certain percentage of headlines. It should probably be included in every advertisement. But those are not things to guess at. They should be decided by actual knowledge, usually by traced returns.

This chapter, like every chapter, points out a very important reason for knowing your results. Scientific advertising is impossible without that. So is safe advertising. So is maximum profit.

Groping in the dark in this field has probably cost enough money to pay the national debt. That is what has filled the advertising graveyards. That is what has discouraged thousands who could profit in this field. And the dawn of knowledge is what is bringing a new day in the advertising world.

Chapter Eleven

Information

An ad-writer, to have a chance at success, must gain full information on his subject. The library of an ad agency should have books on every line that calls for research. A painstaking advertising man will often read for weeks on some problem which comes up.

Perhaps in many volumes he will find few facts to use. But some one fact may be the keynote of success.

This writer has just completed an enormous amount of reading, medical and otherwise, on coffee. This to advertise a coffee without caffeine.

One scientific article out of a thousand perused gave the keynote for that campaign. It was the fact that caffeine stimulation comes two hours after drinking. So the immediate bracing effects which people seek from coffee do not come from the caffeine. Removing caffeine does not remove the kick. It does not modify coffee's delights, for caffeine is tasteless and odorless.

Caffeine-less coffee has been advertised for years. People regarded it like near-beer. Only through weeks of reading did we find a way to put it another light.

To advertise a tooth paste this writer has also read many volumes of scientific matter, dry as dust. But in the middle of one volume he found the idea which has helped make millions for that tooth paste maker. And has made this campaign one of the sensations of advertising.

Genius is the art of taking pains. The advertising man who spares the midnight oil will never get very far.

Before advertising a food product, 130 men were employed for weeks to interview all classes of consumers.

On another line, letters we sent to 12,000 physicians. Questionnaires are often mailed to tens of thousands of men and women to get the viewpoint of consumers.

A $25,000-a-year man, before advertising outfits for acetylene gas, spent weeks in going from farm to farm. Another man did that on a tractor.

Before advertising a shaving cream, one thousand men were asked to state what they most desired in a shaving soap.

Called on to advertise pork and beans, a canvass was made of some thousands of homes. There-to-fore all pork and bean advertising has been based on "Buy my brand." That canvass showed that only 4 per cent of the people used any canned pork and beans. Ninety-six per cent baked their beans at home.

The problem was not to sell a particular brand. Any such attempt appealed to only four per cent. The right appeal was to win the people away from home-baked beans. The advertising, which without knowledge must have failed, proved a great success.

A canvass is made, not only of homes, but of dealers. Competition is measured up. Every advertiser of a similar product is written for his literature and claims. Thus we start with exact information on all that are rivals are doing.

Clipping bureaus are patronized, so that everything printed on our subject comes to the man who writes ads. Every comment that comes from consumers or dealers goes to this man's desk.

It is often necessary in a line to learn the total expenditure. We must learn what a user spends a year, else we shall not know if users are worth the cost of getting them. We must learn the total consumption, else we may overspend.

We must learn the percentage of readers to whom our product appeals. We must often gather this data on classes. The percentage may differ on farms and in cities. The cost of advertising largely depends on the percentage of wasted circulation.

Thus an advertising campaign is usually preceded by a very large volume of data. Even an experimental campaign, for effective experiments cost a great deal of work and time.

Often chemists are employed to prove or disprove doubtful claims. An advertiser, in all good faith, makes an impressive assertion. If it is true, it will form a big factor in advertising. If untrue, it may prove a boomerang. And it may bar our ads from good mediums. It is remarkable how often a maker proves wrong on assertions he has made for years.

Impressive claims are made far more impressive by making them exact. So many experiments are made to get the actual figures. For instance, a certain drink is known to have a large food value. That simple assertion is not very convincing.

So we send the drink to the laboratory and find that its food value is 425 calories per pint. One pint is equal to six eggs in calories of nutriment. That claim makes a great impression.

In every line involving scientific details a censor is appointed. The ad-writer, however well informed, may draw wrong inferences from facts. So an authority passes on every advertisement.

The uninformed would be staggered to know the amount of work involved in a single ad. Weeks of work sometimes. The ad seems so simple, and it must be simple to appeal to simple people. But back of that ad may lie reams of data, volumes of information, months of research.

So this is no lazy man's field.

Chapter Twelve

Strategy

Advertising is much like war, minus the venom. Or much, if you prefer, like a game of chess. We are usually out to capture others' citadels or garner others' trade.

We must have skill and knowledge. We must have training and experience, also the right equipment. We must have proper ammunition, and enough. We dare not underestimate opponents. Our intelligence department is a vital factor, as told in the previous chapter.

We need alliances with dealers, as another chapter tells. We also need strategy of the ablest sort, to multiply the value of our forces.

Sometimes in new campaigns comes the question of a name. That may be most important. Often the right name is an advertisement in itself. It may tell a fairly complete story, like Shredded Wheat, Cream of Wheat, Puffed Rice, Spearmint Gum, Palmolive Soap, etc.

That may be a great advantage. The name is usually conspicuously displayed. Many a name has proved to be the greatest factor in an article's success. Other names prove a distinct disadvantage - Toasted Corn Flakes, for instance. Too many others may share a demand with the man who builds it up.

Many coined names without meaning have succeeded. Kodak, Karo etc., are examples. They are exclusive. The advertiser who gives them meaning never needs to share his advantage.

But a significant name which helps to impress a dominant claim is certainly a good advantage. Names that tell stories have been worth millions of dollars. So a great deal of research often precedes the selection of a name.

Sometimes a price must be decided. A high price creates resistance. It tends to limit one's field. The cost of getting the added profit may be more than the profit.

It is a well-known fact that the greatest profits are made on great volume at small profit. Campbell's Soups, Palmolive Soap, Karo Syrup and Ford cars are conspicuous examples. A price which appeals only to, say 10 percent, multiplies the cost of selling.

But on other lines, high price is unimportant. High profit is essential. The line may have small sale per customer. One hardly cares what he pays for a corn remedy because he uses little. The maker must have a large margin because of small consumption.

On other lines, a higher price may even be an inducement. Such lines are judged largely by price. A product which costs more than the ordinary is considered above the ordinary. So the price question is always a very big factor in strategy.

Competition must be considered. What are the forces against you? What have they in price or quality or claims to weigh against your appeal? What have you to win trade against them? What have you to hold trade against them when you get it?

How strongly are your rivals entrenched? There are some fields which are almost impregnable. They are usually lines which create a new habit or custom and which typify that custom with consumers. They so dominate a field that one can hardly hope to invade it. They have volume, the profit to make a tremendous fight.

Such fields are being constantly invaded. But it is done through some convincing advantage, or through very superior salesmanship-in-print.

Other lines are only less difficult. A new shaving soap is an example. About every possible customer is using a rival soap. Most of them are satisfied with it. Many are wedded to it. The appeal must be strong enough to win those people from long-established favor.

Such things are not accomplished by haphazard efforts. Not by considering people in the mass and making blind stabs for their favors.

We must consider individuals, typical people who are using rival brands. A man on a Pullman, for instance, using his favorite soap. What could you say to him in person to get him to change to yours?

We cannot go after thousands of men until we learn how to win one.

The maker may say that he has no distinctions. He is making a good product, but much like others. He deserves a good share of the trade, but he has nothing exclusive to offer.

However, there is nearly always something impressive which others have not told. We must discover it. We must have a seeming advantage. People don't quit habits without a reason.

There is the problem of substitution and how to head it off. That often steals much of one's trade. This must be considered in one's original plan.

One must have foresight to see all eventualities, and the wisdom to establish his defenses in advance.

Many pioneers in the line establish large demands. Then, through some fault in their foundations, lose a large share of the harvest. Theirs is a mere brand, for instance, where it might have stood for an exclusive product.

Vaseline is an example. That product established a new demand, then almost monopolized that demand through wisdom at the start. To have called it some different brand of petroleum jelly might have made a difference of millions in results.

Jell-O, Postum, Victrola, Kodak, etc., established coined names which came to typify a product. Some such names have been admitted to the dictionary. They have become common names, though coined and exclusive.

Royal Baking Powder and Toasted Corn Flakes, on the other hand, when they pioneered their fields, left the way open to perpetual substitution. So did Horlick's Malted Milk.

The attitude of dealers must be considered. There is a growing inclination to limit lines, to avoid duplicate lines, to lesson inventories.

If this applies to your line, how will dealers receive it? If there is opposition, how can we circumvent it?

The problems of distribution are important and enormous. To advertise something that few dealers supply is a waste of ammunition. Those problems will be considered in another chapter.

These are samples of the problems which advertising men must solve. These are some of the reasons why vast experience is necessary. One oversight may cost the client millions in the end. One wrong piece of strategy may prohibit success.

Things done in one way may be twice as easy, half as costly, as when done another way.

Advertising without this preparation is like a waterfall going to waste. The power might be there, but it is not made effective. We must center the force and direct it in a practical direction.

Advertising often looks very simple. Thousands of men claim ability to do it. And there is still is a wide impression that many men can. As a result, much advertising goes by favor.

But the men who know realize that the problems are as many and as important as the problems in building a skyscraper. And many of them lie in the foundations.

Chapter Thirteen

Use of Samples

The product itself should be its own best salesman.

Not the product alone, but the product plus a mental impression, and atmosphere, which you place around it.

That being so, samples of prime importance. However expensive, they usually form the cheapest selling method. A salesman might as well go out without his sample case as an advertiser.

Sampling does not apply to little things alone, like foods or proprietaries. It can be applied in some way to almost everything. We have sampled clothing. We are now sampling phonograph records.

Samples serve numerous valuable purposes. They enable one to use the word "Free" in ads. That often multiplies readers. Most people want to learn about an offered gift. Tests often show that samples pay for themselves - perhaps several times over - in multiplying the readers of your ads without additional cost of space.

A sample gets action. The reader of your ad may not be convinced to the point of buying. But he ready to learn more about the product that you offer. So he cuts out a coupon, lays it aside, and later mails it or presents it. Without that coupon, he would soon forget.

Then you have the name and address of an interested prospect. You can start him using your product. You can give him fuller information. You can follow him up.

That reader might not again read one of your ads in six months. Your impression would be lost. But when he writes you, you have a chance to complete with that prospect all that can be done. In that saving of waste the sample pays for itself.

Sometimes a small sample is not a fair test. Then we may send an order on the dealer for a full-size package. Or we may make the coupon good for a package at the store. Thus we get a longer test.

You say that is expensive. So is it expensive to gain a prospect's interest. It may cost you 50 cents to get the person to the point of writing for a sample. Don't stop at 15 cents additional to make that interest valuable.

Another way in which samples pay is by keying your advertisements.

They register the interest you create. Thus you can compare one with another, the ad, headline, plan and method. That means, in any line, an enormous savings.

The wisest, most experienced man cannot tell what will most appeal in any line of copy. Without a key to guide you, your returns are very apt to cost you twice what they need cost. And we know that some ads on the same product will cost ten times what others cost. A sample may pay for itself several times over by giving you an accurate check.

Again, samples enable you to refer customers where they can be supplied. This is important before you attain general distribution.

Many advertisers lose much by being penny-wise. They are afraid of imposition, or they try to save pennies. That is why they ask ten cents for a sample, or a stamp or two.

Getting that dime may cost them from 40 cents to 1 dollar. That is, it may add that to the cost of replies.

But it is remarkable how many will pay that addition rather than offer a sample free. Putting a price on a sample greatly retards replies. Then it prohibits you from using the word "Free." Free, as we have stated, will generally more than pay for your samples.

For the same reason, some advertisers say, "You buy one package, we will buy the other." Or they make a coupon good for part of the purchase price.

Any keyed returns will clearly prove that such offers do not pay.

Before a prospect is converted, it is approximately as hard to get half price for your article as to get the full price for it.

Bear in mind that you are the seller. You are the one courting interest. Then don't make it difficult to exhibit that interest. Don't ask your prospects to pay for your selling efforts. Three in four will refuse to pay - perhaps nine in ten.

Cost of requests for samples differ in every line. It depends on your breadth of appeal. Some things appeal to everybody, some to a small percentage.

One issue of the papers in Greater New York brought 1,460,000 requests for a can of evaporated milk. On a chocolate drink, one-fifth the coupons published are presented. Another line not widely used may bring a fraction of that number.

But the cost of inquiries is usually enough to be important.

Then don't neglect them. Don't stint your efforts with those you have half sold.

An inquiry means that a prospect has read your story and is interested. He or she would like to try your product and learn more about it. Do what you would do if that prospect stood before you.

Cost of inquiries depends largely on how they come. Asking people to mail the coupon brings minimum returns. Often four times as many will present that coupon for a sample at the store.

On a line before the writer now, sample inquiries obtained by mail average 70 cents each. The same ads bring inquiries at from 18 cents to 22 cents each when the coupons are presented at a local store.

Most people write few letters. Writing is an effort. Perhaps they have no stamps in the house. Most people will pay car-fare to get a sample rather than two cents postage.

Therefore, it is always best, where possible, to have samples delivered locally.

On one line three methods were offered. The woman could write for a sample, or telephone, or call at a store. Seventy per cent of the inquiries came by telephone. The use of the telephone is more common and convenient than the use of stamps.

Sometimes it is not possible to supply all dealers with samples. Then we refer people to some central stores. These stores are glad to have many people come there. And other dealers do not generally object so long as they share in the sales.

It is important to have these dealers send you the coupons promptly. Then you can follow up the inquiries while their interest is fresh.

It is said that sample users repeat. They do to some extent. But repeaters form a small percentage. Figure it in your cost.

Say to the woman, "Only one sample to a home" and few women will try to get more of them. And the few who cheat you are not generally the people who would buy. So you are not losing purchasers, but the samples only.

On numerous lines we have for long offered full-sized packages free. The packages were priced at from 10 cents to 50 cents each. In certain territories for a time we have checked up on repeaters. And we found the loss much less than the cost of checking.

In some lines, samples would be wasted on children, and they are most apt to get them. Then say in your coupon "adults only." Children will not present such coupons, and they will rarely mail them in.

But one must be careful about publishing coupons good for a full-size package at any store. Some people, and even dealers, may buy up many papers. We do not announce the date of such offers. And we insert them in Sunday papers, not so easily bought up.

But we do not advocate samples given out promiscuously. Samples distributed to homes, like waifs on the doorsteps, probably never pay. Many of them never reach the house or the housewife.

When they do, there is no prediction for them. The product is cheapened. It is not introduced in a favorable way.

So with demonstrations in stores. There is always a way to get the same results at a fraction of the cost.

Many advertisers do not understand this. They supply thousands of samples to dealers to be handed out as they will. Could a trace be placed on the cost of returns, the advertiser would be stunned.

Give samples to interested people only. Give them only to people who exhibit that interest by some effort. Give them only to people whom you have told your story.

First create an atmosphere of respect, a desire, an expectation. When people are in that mood, your sample will usually confirm the qualities you claim.

Here again comes the advantage of figuring cost per customer. That is the only way to gauge advertising. Samples sometimes seem to double advertising cost. They often cost more than the advertising.

Yet, rightly used, they almost invariably form the cheapest way to get customers. And that is what you want.

The argument against samples are usually biased. They may come from advertising agents who like to see all the advertising money spent in print.

Answer such arguments by tests. Try some towns with them, some without. Where samples are effectively employed, we rarely find a line where they do not lessen the cost per customer.

Chapter Fourteen

Getting Distribution

Most advertisers are confronted with the problem of getting distribution. National advertising is unthinkable without that. A venture cannot be profitable if nine in ten of the converts fail to find the goods.

To force dealers to stock by bringing repeated demands may be enormously expensive. To cover the country with a selling force is usually impossible. To get dealers to stock an unknown line on promise of advertising is not easy. They have seen too many efforts fail, too many promises rescinded.

We cannot discuss all plans for getting distribution. There are scores of ways employed, according to the enterprise. Some start by soliciting direct sales, mail orders, until the volume of demand forces dealers to supply. Some get into touch with prospects by a sample or other offer, and then refer them to certain dealers who are stocked.

Some well-known can get a large percentage of dealers to stock in advance under guarantee of sale. Some consign goods to jobbers so dealers can easily order. Some name certain dealers in their ads until dealers in general stock.

The problems in this line are numberless. The successful methods are many. But most of them apply to lines too few to be worthy of discussion in a book like this.

We shall deal here with articles of wide appeal and repeated sales, like foods or proprietary articles. We usually start with local advertising, even though magazine advertising is best adapted to the article. We get our distribution town by town, then change to national advertising.

Sometimes we name the dealers who are stocked. As others stock, we add their names. When a local campaign is proposed, naming certain dealers, the average dealer wants to be included. It is often possible to get most of them by offering to name them in the first few ads.

Whether you advertise few or many dealers, the others will stock in very short order if the advertising is successful. Then the trade is referred to all dealers.

The sample plans dealt with in the previous chapter aid quick distribution. They often pay for themselves in this way alone.

If the samples are distributed locally, the coupon names the store. The prospects who go there to get the samples know that those stores are supplied, if a nearer dealer is not. Thus little trade is lost.

When sample inquiries come to the advertiser, inquiries are referred to certain dealers at the start. Enough demand is centered there to force those dealers to supply it.

Sometimes most stores are supplied with samples, but on the requirement of a certain purchase. You supply a dozen samples with a dozen packages, for instance. Then inquiries for samples are referred to all stores. This quickly forces general distribution. Dealers don't like to have their customers go to competitors, even for a sample.

Where a coupon is used, good at any store for a full-size package, the problem of distribution becomes simple. Mail to dealers proofs of the ad which will contain a coupon. Point out to each that many of his customers are bound to present that coupon. Each coupon presents a cash sale at full profit. No average dealer will let those coupon customers go elsewhere.

Such a free-package offer often pays for itself in this way. It forms the cheapest way of getting general distribution. Some of the most successful advertisers have done this in a national way.

They have inserted coupon ads in magazines, each coupon good at any store for a full-size package. A proof of the ad is sent to dealers in advance, with a list of the magazines to be used, and their circulation.

In this way, in one week sometimes, makers attain a reasonable national distribution. And the coupon ad, when it appears, completes it.

Here again the free packages cost less than other ways of forcing distribution. And they start thousands of users, besides. Palmolive Soap and Puffed Grains are among the products which attain their distribution in that way.

Half the circulation of a newspaper may go to outside towns. That half may be wasted if you offer a sample at local stores.

Say in your coupon that outside people should write you for a sample. When they write, do not mail the sample. Send the samples to a local store, and refer inquiries to that store. Mailing a sample may make a convert who cannot be supplied. But the store which supplies the sample will usually supply demand.

In these ways, many advertisers get national distribution without employing a single salesman. They get it immediately. And they get it at far lower cost that by any other method.

There are advertisers who, in starting, send every dealer a few packages as a gift. That is better, perhaps, than losing customers created. But it is very expensive.

Those free packages must be sold by advertising. Figure their cost at your selling price, and you will see that you are paying a high cost per dealer. A salesman might sell these small stocks at a lower cost. And other methods might be vastly cheaper.

Sending stocks on consignment to retailers is not widely favored. Many dealers resent it. Collections are difficult. And business-like methods do not win dealer respect.

The plans advocated here are the best plans yet discovered for the lines to which they apply. Other lines require different methods. The ramifications are too many to discuss in a book like this.

But don't start advertising without distribution. Don't get distribution by methods too expensive, or by slow, old-fashioned methods.

The loss of time may cost you enormously in sales. And it may enable energetic rivals to get ahead of you.

Go to men who know by countless experiences the best plan to apply to your line.

Chapter Fifteen

Test Campaigns

Almost any questions can be answered, cheaply, quickly and finally, by a test campaign. And that's the way to answer them - not by arguments around a table. Go to the court of last resort - the buyers of your product.

On every new project there comes up the question of selling that article profitably. You and your friends may like it, but the majority may not.

Some rival product may be better liked or cheaper. It may be strongly entrenched. The users won away from it may cost too much to get. People may buy and not repeat. The article may last too long. It may appeal to a small percentage, so most of your advertising goes to waste.

There are many surprises in advertising. A project you will laugh at may make a great success. A project you are sure of may fall down. All because tastes differ so. None of us know enough people's desires to get an average viewpoint.

In the old days, advertisers ventured on their own opinions. The few guessed right, the many wrong. Those were the times of advertising disaster.

Even those who succeeded came close to the verge before the time is turned. They did not know their cost per customer or their sale per customer. The cost of selling might take a long to come back. Often, it never came back.

Now we let the thousands decide what the millions will do.

We make a small venture, and watch cost and result. When we learn what a thousand customers cost, we know almost exactly what a million will cost. When we learn what they buy, we know what a million will buy.

We establish averages on a small scale, and those averages always hold. We know our cost, we know our sale, we know our profit and loss. We know how soon our cost comes back.

Before we spread out, we prove our undertaking absolutely safe. So there are today, no advertising disasters piloted by men who know.

Perhaps we try out our project in four or five towns. We may use a sample offer or a free package to get users started quickly.

Then we wait and see if users buy those samples. If they do, will they continue? How much will they buy? How long does it take for the profit to return our cost of selling?.

A test like this may cost $3,000 to $5,000. It is not all lost, even when the product proves unpopular. Some sales are made. Nearly every test will, in time, bring back the entire cost.

Sometimes we find that the cost of the advertising comes back before the bills are due. That means that the product can be advertised without investment. Many a great advertiser has been built up without any cost whatever beyond immediate receipts. That is an ideal situation.

On another product it may take three months to bring back the cost with a profit. But one is sure of his profit in that time. When he spreads out, he must finance accordingly.

Think what this means. A man has what he considers an advertising possibility. But national advertising looks so big and expensive that he dare not undertake it.

Now he presents it in a few average towns, at a very moderate cost. With almost no risk whatever. From the few thousands, he learns what the millions will do. Then he acts accordingly. If he then branches out, he knows to a certainty just what his results will be.

He is playing on the safe side of a hundred to one shot. If the article is successful, it may make him millions. If he is mistaken about it, the loss is a trifle.

These are facts we desire to emphasize and spread. All our largest accounts are now built in this way, from very small beginnings. When business men realize that this can be done, hundreds of others will do it. For countless fortune-earners now lie dormant.

The largest advertiser in the world makes a business of starting such projects. One by one he finds out winners. Now he has twenty-six, and together they earn many millions yearly.

These test campaigns have other purposes. They answer countless questions which arise in business.

A large food advertiser felt that his product would be more popular in another form. He and all his advisers were certain about it. They were willing to act on this supposition without consulting the consumers, but wiser advice prevailed.

He inserted an ad in a few towns with a coupon, good at any store for a package of the new-style product. Then he wrote to the users about it. They were almost unanimous in their disapproval.

Later the same product was suggested in still another form. The previous verdict made the change look dubious. The advertiser hardly thought a test to be worthwhile.

But he submitted the question to a few thousand women in a similar way and 91 per cent voted for it. Now he has a unique product which promises to largely increase his sales.

These tests cost about $1,000 each. The first one saved him a very costly mistake. The second will probably bring him large profits.

Then we try test campaigns to try out new methods on advertising already successful. Thus we constantly seek for better methods, without interrupting plans already proved out.

In five years for one food advertiser we tried out over fifty separate plans. Every little while we found an improvement, so the results of our advertising constantly grew.

At the end of five years we found the best plan of all. It reduced our cost of selling by 75 per cent. That is, it was four times more effective than the best plan used before.

That is what mail order advertisers do - try out plan after plan to constantly reduce the cost. Why should any general advertiser be less business-like and careful?

Another service of the test campaign is this:

An advertiser is doing mediocre advertising. A skilled advertising agent feels that he can greatly increase results. The advertiser is doubtful. He is doing fairly well. He has alliances which he hesitates to break. So he is inclined to let well enough alone.

Now the question can be submitted to the verdict of a test. The new agent may take a few towns, without interfering with the general campaign. Then compare his results with the general results and prove his greater skill.

Plausible arguments are easy in this line. One man after another comes to an advertiser to claim superior knowledge or ability. It is hard to decide, and decisions may be wrong.

Now actual figures gained at a small cost can settle the question definitely. The advertiser makes no commitment. It is like saying to a salesman, "Go out for a week and prove."

A large percentage of all the advertising done would change hands if this method were applied. Again we come back to scientific advertising.

Suppose a chemist would say in an arbitrary way that this compound was best, or that better. You would little respect his opinion.

He makes tests - sometimes hundreds of tests - to actually know which is best. He will never state a supposition before he has proved it.

How long before advertisers in general will apply that exactness to advertising?

Chapter Sixteen

Leaning on Dealers

We cannot depend much in most lines on the active help of jobbers or of dealers. They are busy. They have many lines to consider. The profit on advertised lines is not generally large. And an advertised article is apt to be sold at cut prices.

The average dealer does what you would do. He exerts himself on brands of his own, if at all. Not on another man's brand.

The dealer will often try to make you think otherwise. He will ask some aid or concession on the ground of extra effort.

Advertisers often give extra discounts. Or they make loading offers - perhaps one case free in ten - in the belief that loaded dealers will make extra efforts.

This may be so rare lines, but not generally. And the efforts if made do not usually increase the total sales. They merely swing trade from one store to another.

On most lines, making a sale without making a convert does not count for much. Sales made by conviction - by advertising - are likely to bring permanent customers.

People who buy through casual recommendations do not often stick. Next time someone else gives other advice.

Revenue which belongs to the advertiser is often given away without adequate return. These discounts and gifts could be far better spent in securing new customers.

Free goods must be sold, and by your own efforts usually.

One extra case with ten means that advertising must sell ten per cent more to bring you the same return. The dealer would probably buy just as much if you let him buy as conveniently.

Much money is often frittered away on other forms of dealer help. Perhaps on window or store displays. A window display, acting as a reminder, may bring to one dealer a lion's share of the trade. Yet it may not increase your total sales at all.

Those are facts to find out. Try one town in one way, one in another. Compare total sales in those towns. In many lines such tests will show that costly displays are worthless. A growing number of experienced advertisers spend no money on displays.

This is all in line of general publicity, so popular long ago. Casting bread upon the waters and hoping for its return. Most advertising was of that sort twenty years ago.

Now we put things to the test. We compare cost and result on every form of expenditure. It is very easily done. Very many costly wastes are eliminated by this modern process.

Scientific advertising has altered many old plans and conceptions. It has proved many long-established methods to be folly. And why should we not apply to these things the same criterion we apply to other forms of selling? Or to manufacturing costs?

Your object in all advertising is to buy new customers at a price which pays a profit. You have no interest in garnering trade at any particular store. Learn what your consumers cost and what they buy. If they cost you one dollar each, figure that every wasted dollar costs you a possible customer.

Your business will be built in that way, not by dealer help.

You must do your own selling, make your own success. Be content if dealers fill the orders that you bring. Eliminate your wastes. Spend all your ammunition where it counts for most.

Chapter Seventeen

Individuality

A person who desires to make an impression must stand out in some way. Being eccentric, being abnormal is not distinction to covet. But doing admirable things in a different way gives one a great advantage.

So with salesman, in person or in print.

There is uniqueness which belittles and arouses resentment. There is refreshing uniqueness which enhances which we welcome and remember. Fortunate is the salesman who has it.

We try to give each advertiser a becoming style. We make him distinctive, perhaps not in appearance, but in manner and in tone. He is given an individuality best suited to the people he addresses.

One man appears rugged and honest in a line where rugged honesty counts. One may be a good fellow where choice is a matter of favor. In other lines the man stands out by impressing himself as an authority.

We have already cited a case where a woman made a great success in selling clothing to girls, solely through a created personality which won their trust.

That's why we have signed ads sometimes - to give them a personal authority. A man is talking - a man who takes pride in his accomplishments - not a "soul-less corporation."

Whenever possible we introduce a personality into our ads. By making a man famous we make his product famous. When we claim an improvement, naming the man who made it adds effect. Then we take care not to change an individuality which has proved appealing.

Before a man writes a new ad on that line, he gets into the spirit adopted by the advertiser. He plays a part as an actor plays it.

In successful advertising great pains are taken to never change our tone. That which won so many is probably the best way to win others. Then people come to know us. We build on that acquaintance rather than introduce a stranger in strange guise. People do not know us by name alone, but by looks and mannerisms. Appearing different every time we meet never builds up confidence.

Then we don't want people to think that salesmanship is made to order. That our appeals are created, studied, artificial. They must seem to come from the heart, and the same heart always, save where a wrong tack forces a complete change.

There are winning personalities in ads as well as people. To some we are glad to listen, others bore us. Some are refreshing, some commonplace. Some inspire confidence, some caution.

To create the right individuality is a supreme accomplishment. Then an advertiser's growing reputation on that line brings him ever-increasing prestige.

Never weary of that part. Remember that a change in our characteristics would compel our best friends to get acquainted all over.

Chapter Eighteen

Negative Advertising

To attack a rival is never good advertising. Don't point out others' faults. It is not permitted in the best mediums. It is never good policy. The selfish purpose is apparent. It looks unfair, not sporty.

If you abhor knockers, always appear a good fellow.

Show a bright side, the happy and attractive side, not the dark and uninviting side of things. Show beauty, not homeliness; health, not sickness.

Don't show the wrinkles you propose to remove, but the face as it will appear. Your customers know all about the wrinkles.

In advertising a dentifrice, show pretty teeth, not bad teeth. Talk of coming good conditions, not conditions which exist. In advertising clothes, picture well-dressed people, not the shabby. Picture successful men, not failures, when you advertise a business course.

Picture what others wish to be, not what they may be now.

We are attracted by sunshine, beauty, happiness, health, success. Then point the way to them, not the way out of the opposite.

Picture envied people, not the envious. Tell people what to do, not what to avoid. Make your every ad breath good cheer. We always dodge a "Lugubrious Blue."

Assume that people will do what you ask.

Say, "Send now for this sample. Don't say, "Why do you neglect this offer?"

That suggests that people are neglecting. Invite them to follow the crowd.

Compare the results of two ads, one negative, one positive. One presenting the dark side, one the bright side. One warning, the other inviting. You will be surprised. You will find that the positive ad out pulls the other four to one, if you have our experience.

The "Before and after taking" ads are follies of the past. They never had a place save with the afflicted. Never let their memory lead you to picture the gloomy side of things.

Chapter Nineteen

Letter Writing

This is another phase of advertising which all of us have to consider. It enters, or should enter, into all campaigns. Every business man receives a large number of circular letters. Most of them go direct to the waste basket. But he acts on others, and others are filed for reference.

Analyze those letters. The ones you act on or the ones you keep have a headline which attracted your interest. At a glance they offer something that you want, something you may wish to know.

Remember that point in all advertising.

A certain buyer spends $50,000,000 per year. Every letter, every circular which comes to his desk gets its deserved attention. He wants information on the lines he buys.

But we have often watched him. In one minute a score of letters may drop into the waste basket. Then one is laid aside. That is something to consider at once. Another is filed under the heading "Varnish." And later when he buys varnish that letter will turn up.

That buyer won several prizes by articles on good buying. His articles were based on information. Yet the great masses of matter which came to him never got more than a glance.

The same principles apply to all advertising. Letter writers overlook them just as advertisers do. They fail to get the right attention. They fail to tell what buyers wish to know.

One magazine sends out millions of letters annually. Some to get subscriptions, some to sell books. Before the publisher sends out five million letters he puts a few thousands to test.

He may try twenty-five letters, each with a thousand prospects. He learns what results will cost. Perhaps the plan is abandoned because it appears unprofitable. If not, the letter which pays best is the letter that he uses.

Just as men are doing now in all scientific advertising.

Mail order advertisers do likewise. They test their letters as they test their ads. A general letter is never used until it proves itself best among many actual returns.

Letter writing has much to do with advertising. Letters to inquirers, follow-up letters. Wherever possible they should be tested. Where that is not possible, they should be based on knowledge gained by tests.

We find the same difference in letters as in ads. Some get action, some do not. Some complete a sale, some forfeit the impression gained. These are letters, going usually to half-made converts, are tremendously important.

Experience generally shows that a two-cent letter gets no more attention than a one-cent letter. Fine stationary no more than poor stationery. The whole appeal lies in the matter.

A letter which goes to an inquirer is like a salesman going to an interested prospect. You know what created that interest. Then follow it up along that line, not on some different argument.

Complete the impression already created. Don't undertake another guess.

Do something if possible to get immediate action. Offer some inducement for it. Or tell what delay may cost. Note how many successful selling letters place a limit on an offer. It expires on a certain date.

That is all done to get prompt decision, to overcome the tendency to delay.

A mail order advertiser offered a catalog. The inquirer might send for three or four similar catalogs. He had that competition in making a sale.

So he wrote a letter when he sent his catalog, and enclosed a personal card. He said,

"You are a new customer, and we want to make you welcome. So when you send your order please enclose this card. The writer wants to see that you get a gift with the order - something you can keep."

With an old customer he gave some other reason for the gift. The offer aroused curiosity. It gave preference to his catalog. Without some compelling reason for ordering elsewhere, the woman sent the order to him. The gift paid for itself several times over by bringing larger sales per catalog.

The ways for getting action are many. Rarely can one way be applied to two lines. But the principles are universal. Strike while the iron is hot. Get a decision then. Have it followed by prompt action when you can.

You can afford to pay for prompt action rather than lose by delay.

One advertiser induced hundreds of thousands of women to buy six packages of his product and send him the trademarks, to secure a premium offer good only for one week.

Chapter Twenty

A Name that Helps

There is great advantage in a name that tells a story. The name is usually prominently displayed. To justify the space it occupies, it should aid the advertising.

Some such names are almost complete advertisements in themselves. May Breath is such a name. Cream of Wheat is another. That name alone has been worth a fortune. Other examples are Dutch Cleanser, Cuticura, Dynashine, Minute Tapioca, 3-in-One Oil, Holeproof, Alcorub, Etc. Such names may be protected, yet the name itself describes the product, so it makes a valuable display.

Other coined names are meaningless. Some examples are Kodak, Karo, Sapolio, Vaseline, Kotex, Lux, Postum, etc. They can be protected, and long-continued advertising may give them a meaning. When this is accomplished they become very valuable. But the great majority of them never attain status.

Such names do not aid the advertising. It is very doubtful that they justify display.

The service of the product, not the name, is the important thing in advertising. A vast amount of space is wasted in displaying names and pictures which tell no selling story. The tendency of modern advertising is to eliminate waste.

Other coined names signify ingredients which anyone may use. Examples are Syrup of Figs, Coconut Oil Shampoo, Tar Soap, Palmolive Soap, etc. Such products may dominate a market if the price is reasonable, but they must, to a degree, meet competition. They invite substitution. They are naturally classified with other products which have like ingredients, so the price must remain in that class.

Toasted Corn Flakes and Malted Milk are examples of unfortunate names. In each of those cases one advertiser created a new demand. When the demand was created, others shared it because they could use the name. The originators depended only on a brand.

It is interesting to speculate on how much more profitable a coined name might have been.

On a patented product it must be remembered that the right to a name expires with that patent. Names like Castoria, Aspirin, Shredded Wheat Biscuit, etc., have become common property. This is a very serious point to consider. It often makes a patent an undesirable protection.

Another serious fault in coined names is frivolity. In seeking uniqueness one gets something trivial. And that is a fatal handicap in a serious product. It almost prohibits respect.

When a product must be called by a common name, the best auxiliary name is a man's name. It is much better than a coined name, for it shows that some man is proud of his creation.

Thus the question of a name is of serious importance in laying the foundations of a new undertaking. Some names have become the chief factors in success. Some have lost for their originators four-fifths of the trade they developed.

Chapter Twenty-One

Good Business

A rapid stream ran by the writer's boyhood home. The stream turned a wooden wheel and the wheel ran a mill. Under that primitive method, all but a fraction of the stream's potentiality went to waste.

Then someone applied scientific methods to that stream - put in a turbine and dynamos. Now, with no more water, no more power, it runs a large manufacturing plant.

We think of that stream when we see wasted advertising power. And we see it everywhere - hundreds of examples. Enormous potentialities - millions of circulation - used to turn a mill-wheel. While other use that same power with manifold effect.

We see countless ads running year after year which we know to be unprofitable. Men spending five dollars to do what one dollar might do. Men getting back 30 per cent of their cost when they might get 150 per cent. And the facts could be easily proved.

We see wasted space, frivolity, clever conceits, and entertainment. Costly pages filled with palaver which, if employed by salesman, would reflect on his sanity. But those ads are always unkeyed. The money is spent blindly, merely to satisfy some advertising whim.

Not new advertisers only. Many an old advertiser has little or no idea of his advertising results. The business is growing through many efforts combined, and advertising is given its share of the credit.

An advertiser of many years' standing, spending as high as $700,000 per year, told the writer he did not know whether his advertising was worth anything or not. Sometimes he thought that his business would be just as large without it.

The writer replied, "I do know. Your advertising is utterly unprofitable, and I could prove it to you next week. End an ad with an offer to pay five dollars to anyone who writes you that he read the ad through. The scarcity of replies will amaze you."

Think what a confession - that millions of dollars are being spent without knowledge of results. Such a policy applied to all factors in a business would bring ruin short order.

You see other ads which you may not like as well. They may seem crowded or verbose. They are not attractive to you, for you are seeking something to admire, something to entertain.

But you will note that those ads are keyed. The probability is that out of scores of traced ads the type which you see has paid the best.

Many other ads which are not keyed now were keyed at the beginning. They are based on known statistics. They won on a small scale before they ever ran on large scale. Those advertisers are utilizing their enormous powers in full.

Advertising is prima facie evidence that the man who pays believes that advertising is good. It has brought great results to others, it must be good for him. So he takes it like some secret tonic which others have endorsed. If the business thrives, the tonic gets credit. Otherwise, the failure is due to fate.

That seems almost unbelievable. Even a storekeeper who inserts a twenty-dollar ad knows whether it pays or not. Every line of a big store's ad is charged to the proper department. And every inch used must the next day justify its cost.

Yet most national advertising is done without justification. It is merely presumed to pay. A little test might show a way to multiply returns.

Such methods, still so prevalent, are not very far from their end. The advertising men who practice them see the writing on the wall. The time is fast coming when men who spend money are going to know what they get.

Good business and efficiency will be applied to advertising. Men and methods will be measured by the known returns, and only competent men can survive.

Only one hour ago an old advertising man said to the writer, "The day for our type is done. Bunk has lost its power. Sophistry is being displaced by actuality. And I tremble at the trend."

So do hundreds tremble. Enormous advertising is being done along scientific lines. Its success is common knowledge. Advertisers along other lines will not much longer be content.

We who can meet the test welcome these changed conditions. Advertisers will multiply when they see that advertising can be safe and sure. Small expenditures made on a guess will grow to big ones on a certainty.

Our line of business will be finer, cleaner, when the gamble is removed. And we shall be prouder of it when we are judged on merit.